ROYAL LOCALS
IN LOCKDOWN 2020

Ian Hargreaves

© 2020 Ian Hargreaves. All rights reserved.

No part of this book may be reproduced, stored in a retrieval system, or transmitted by any means without the written permission of the author.

AuthorHouse™ UK
1663 Liberty Drive
Bloomington, IN 47403 USA
www.authorhouse.co.uk
UK TFN: 0800 0148641 (Toll Free inside the UK)
UK Local: 02036 956322 (+44 20 3695 6322 from outside the UK)

Because of the dynamic nature of the Internet, any web addresses or links contained in this book may have changed since publication and may no longer be valid. The views expressed in this work are solely those of the author and do not necessarily reflect the views of the publisher, and the publisher hereby disclaims any responsibility for them.

This book is printed on acid-free paper.

ISBN: 978-1-6655-8105-9 (sc)
ISBN: 978-1-6655-8104-2 (e)

Print information available on the last page.

Published by AuthorHouse 10/14/2020

authorHOUSE®

ROYAL LOCALS
IN LOCKDOWN 2020

Ian Hargreaves

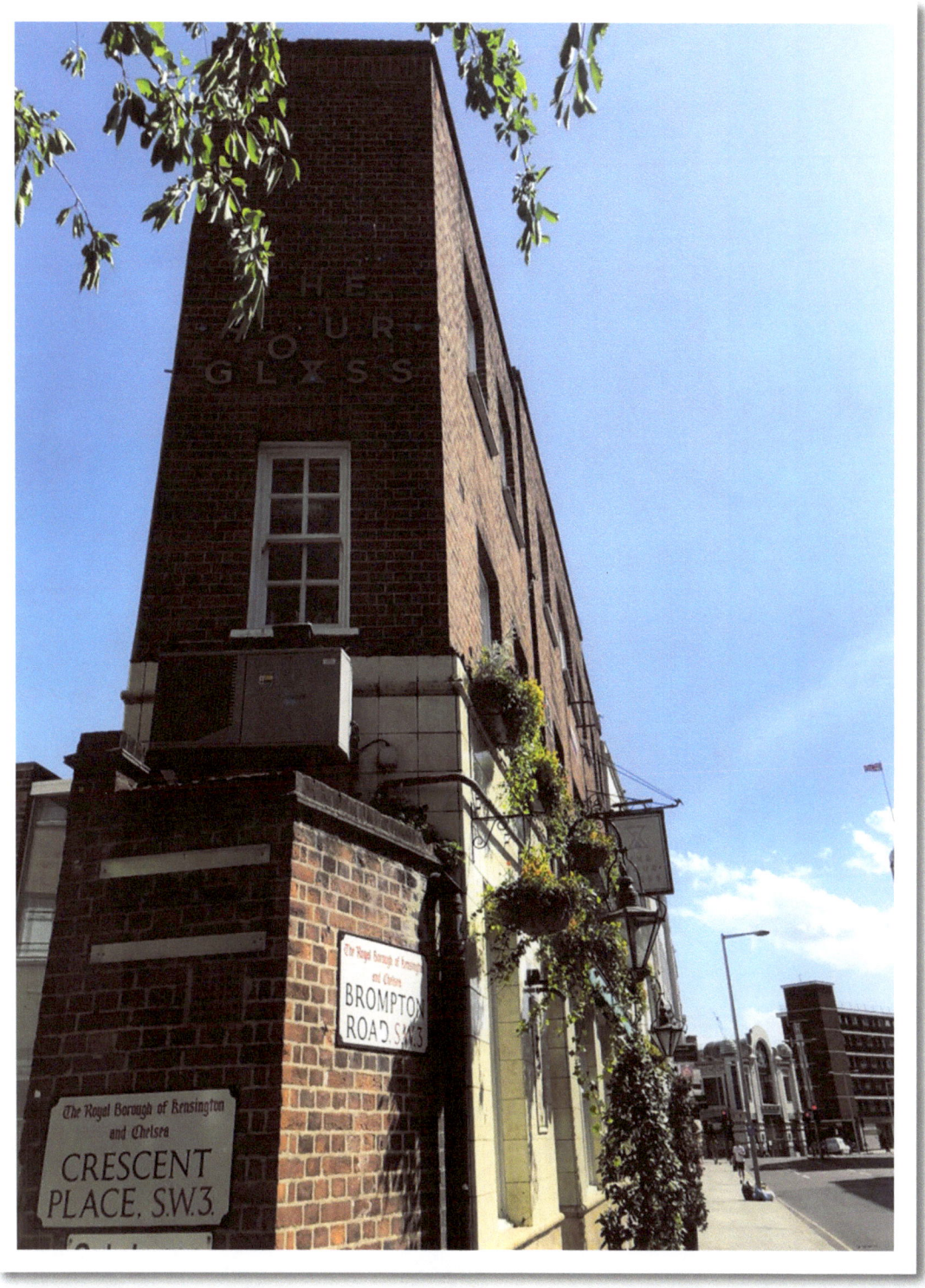

Hour Glass Pub. Many a pint sank in here.

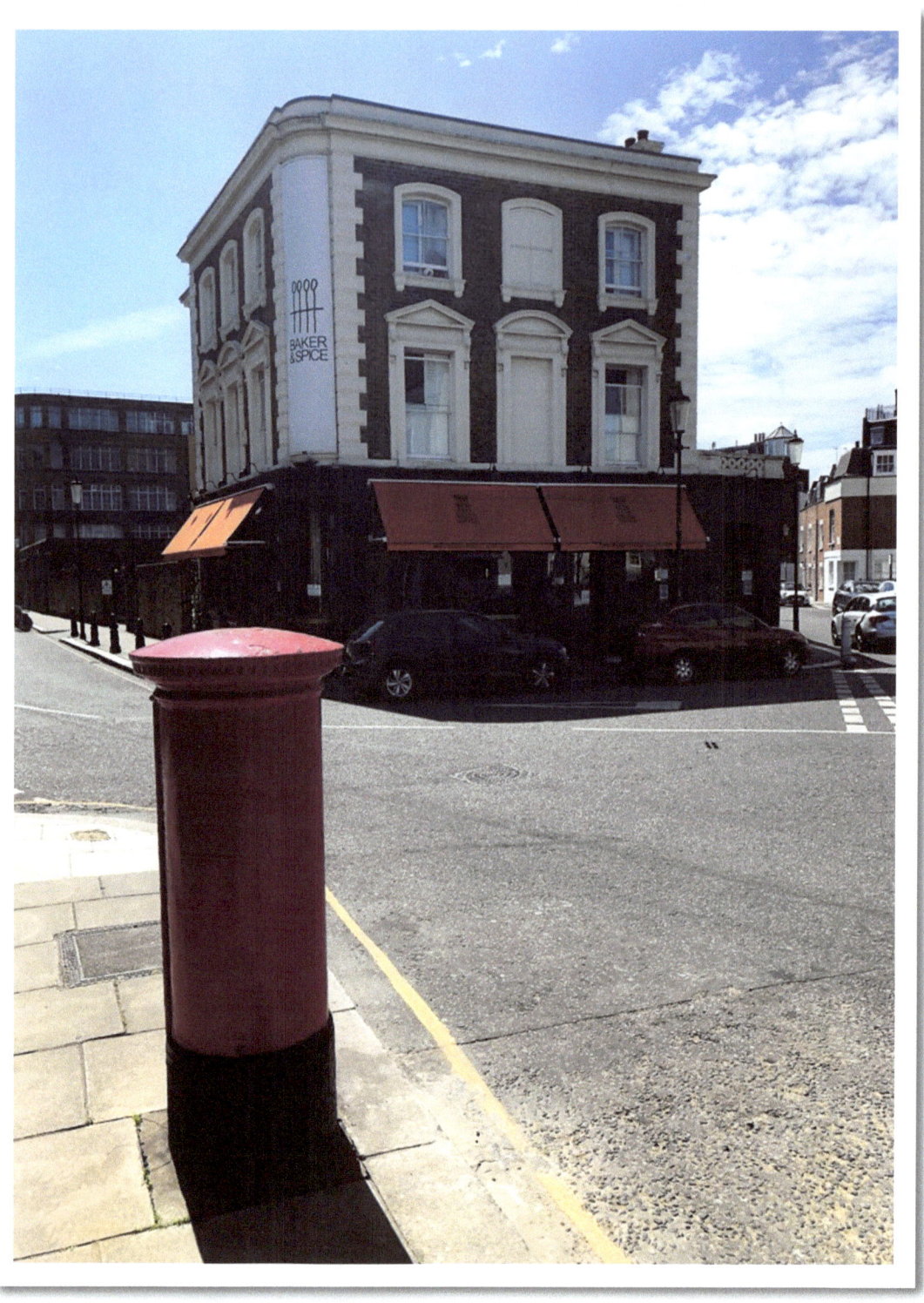

Former Shuckborough Arms now a coffee shop.

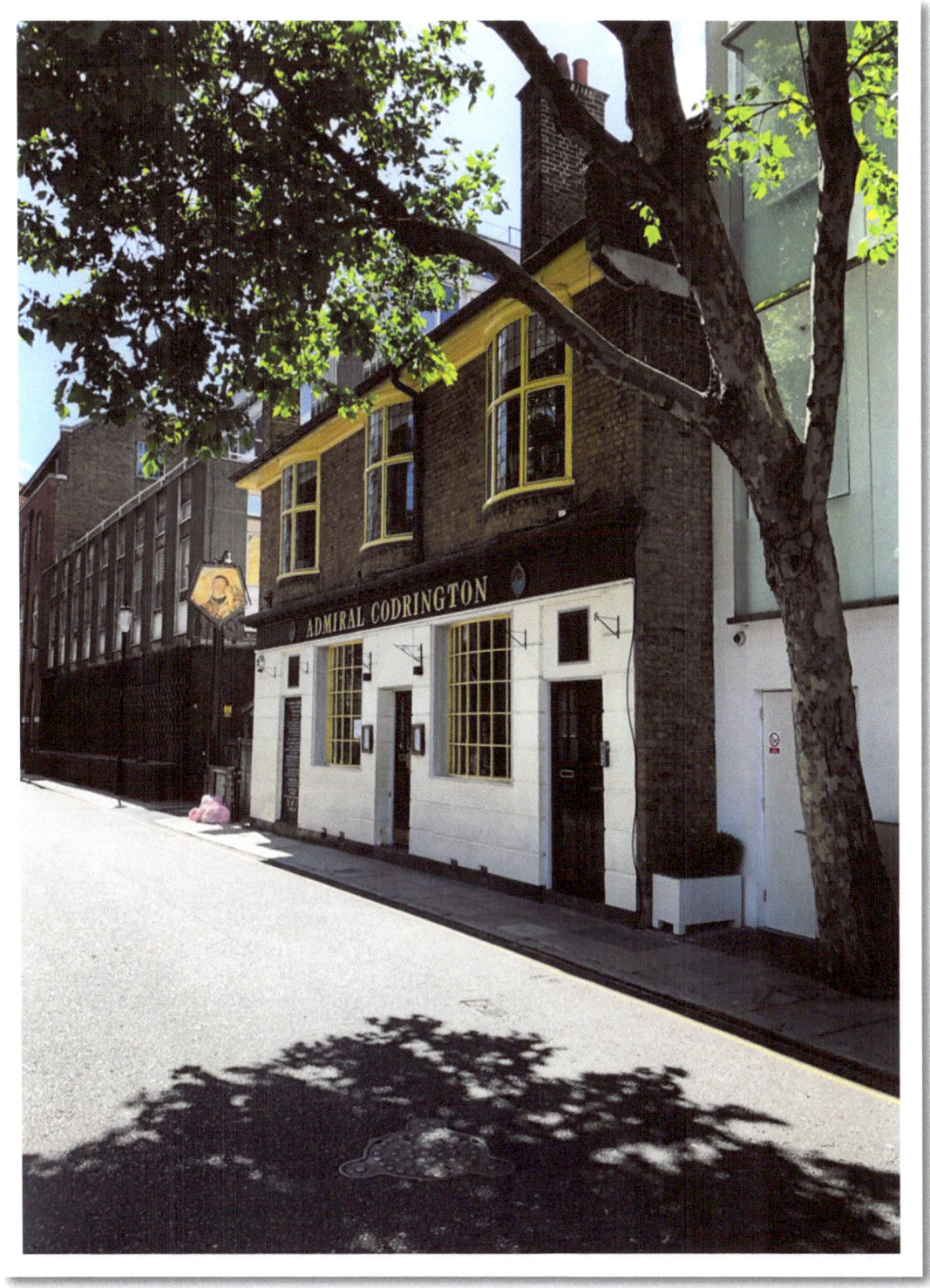

Admiral Codrington Pub. Deepest Chelsea backstreets.

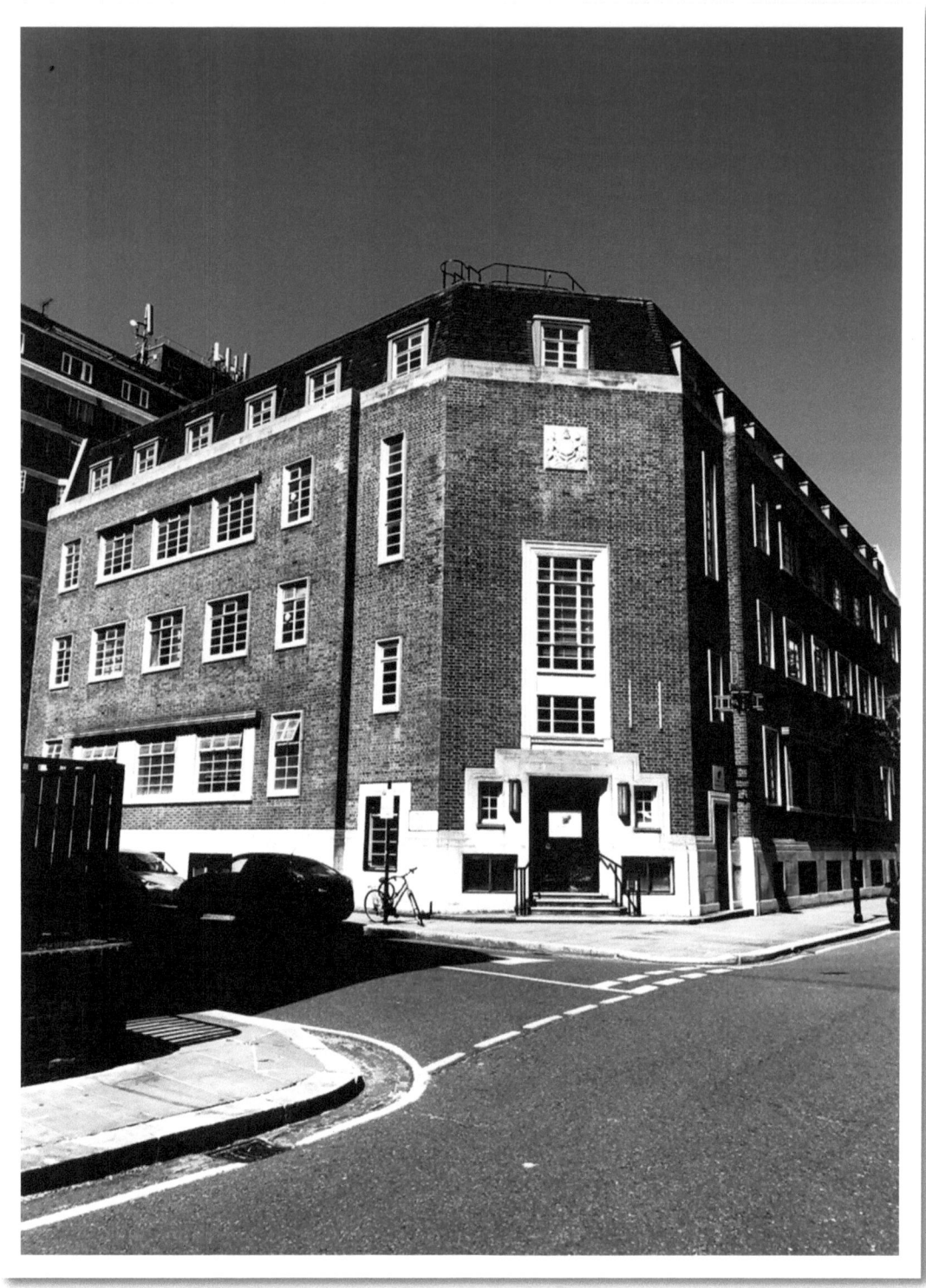

Chelsea Police Station. I was there from 1983 till 1987. Now closed.

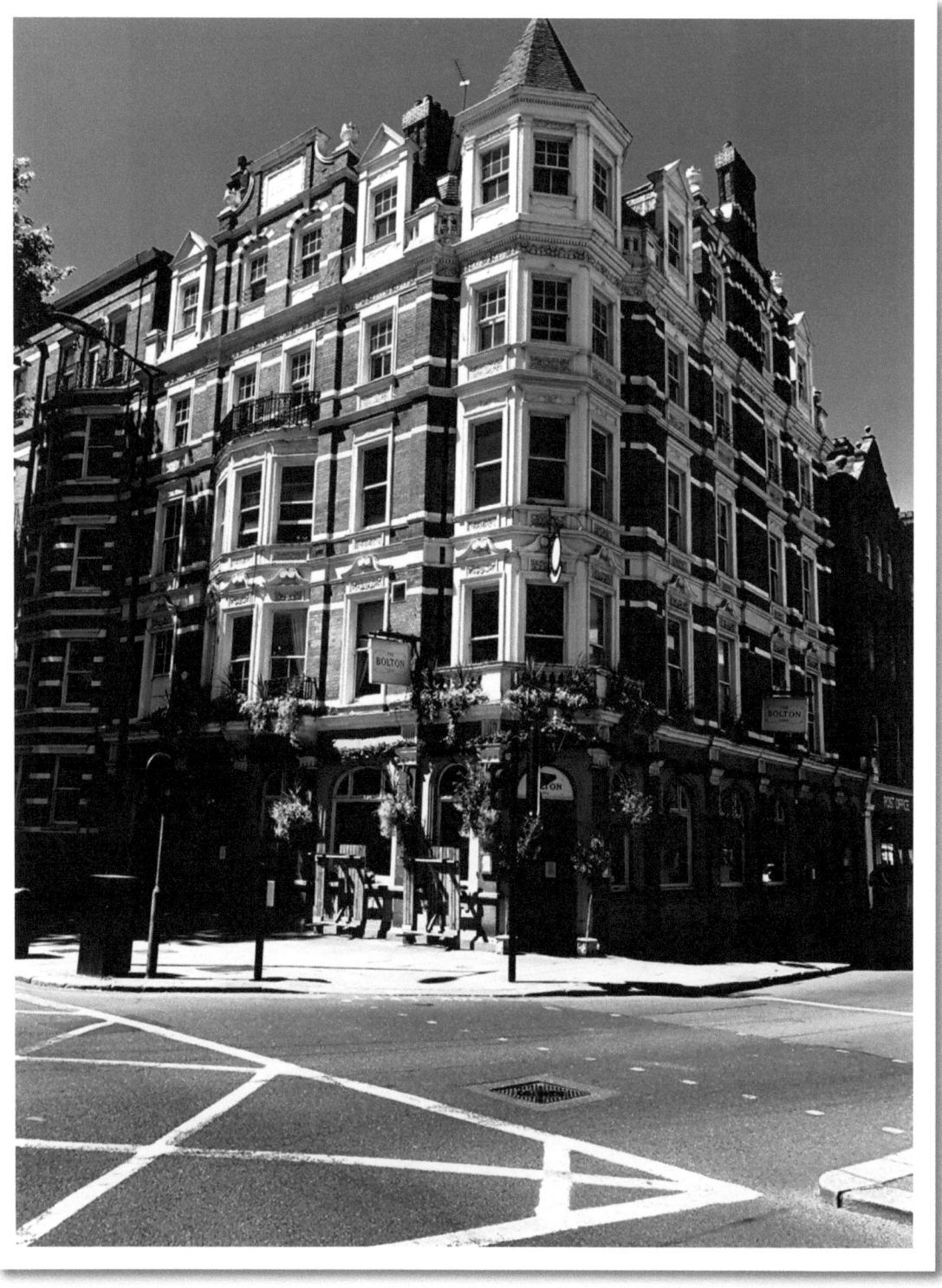

The Bolton. Earls Court Rd. Live Music.

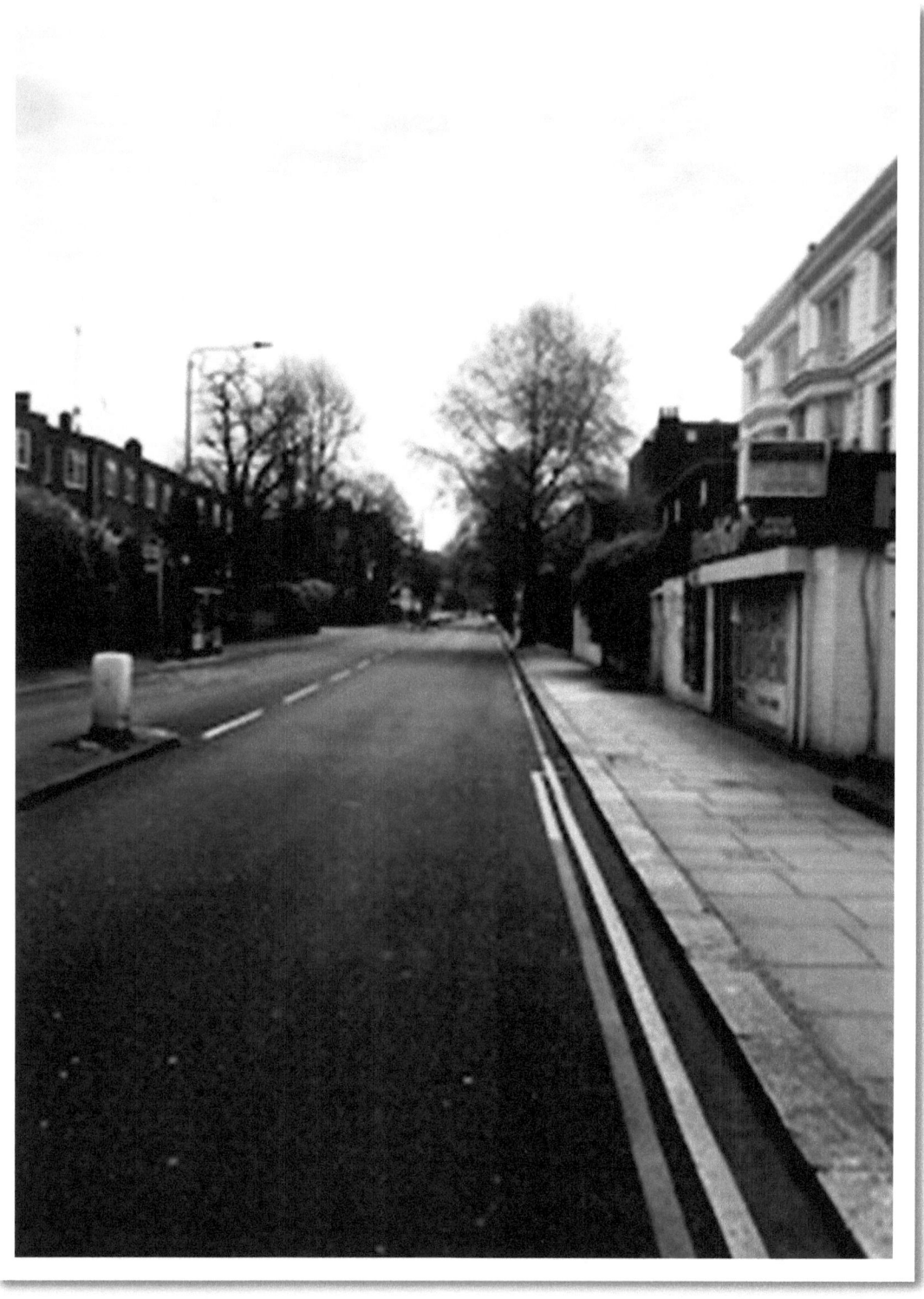

Holland Rd looking South from Russell Gardens W14 at lunch time. Usually a very busy road.

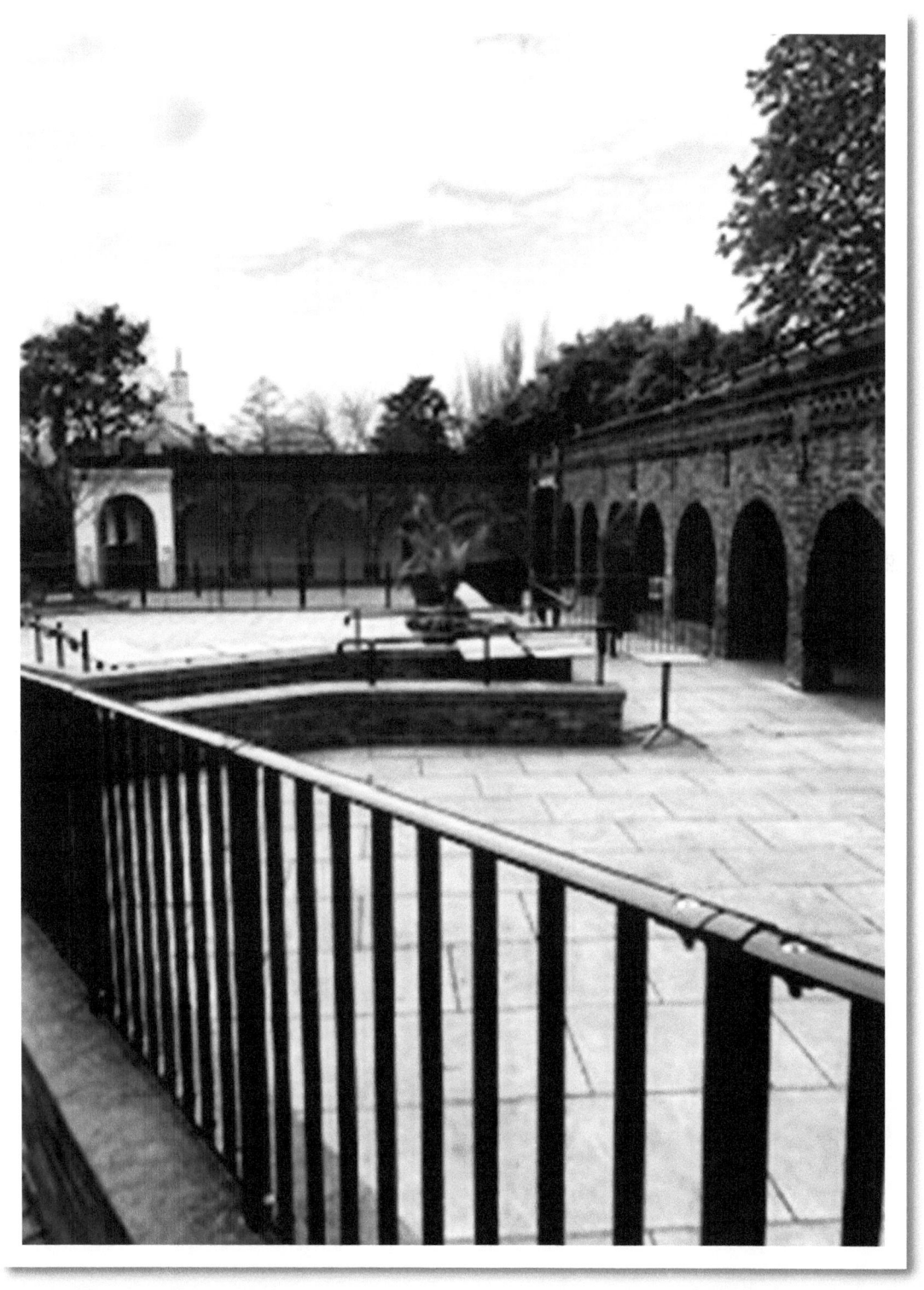

Cafe. Holland Park taken 08/04/20 closed because of COVID.

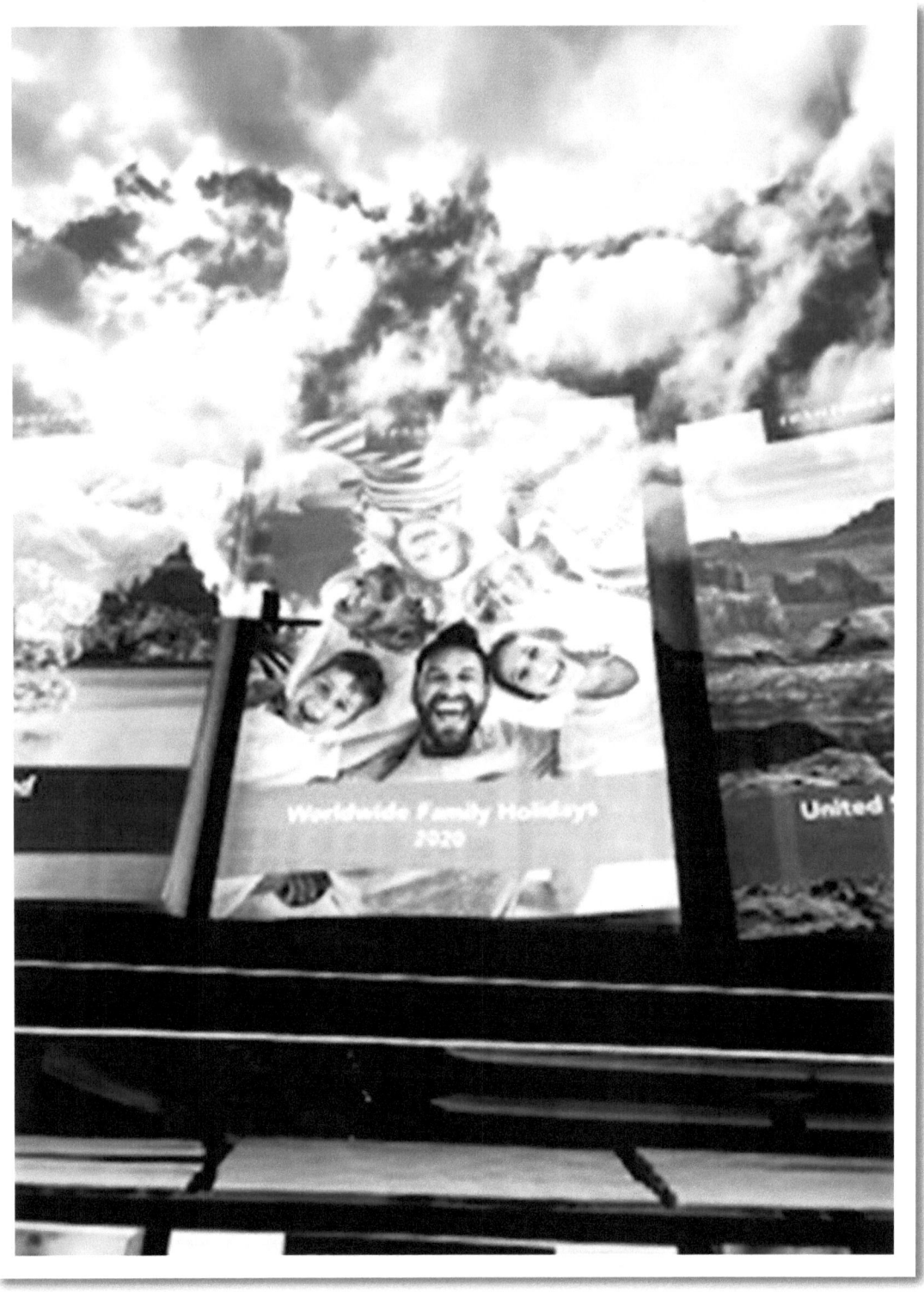

Kensington High Street Travel shop window reflecting clouds. No family holidays in 2020.

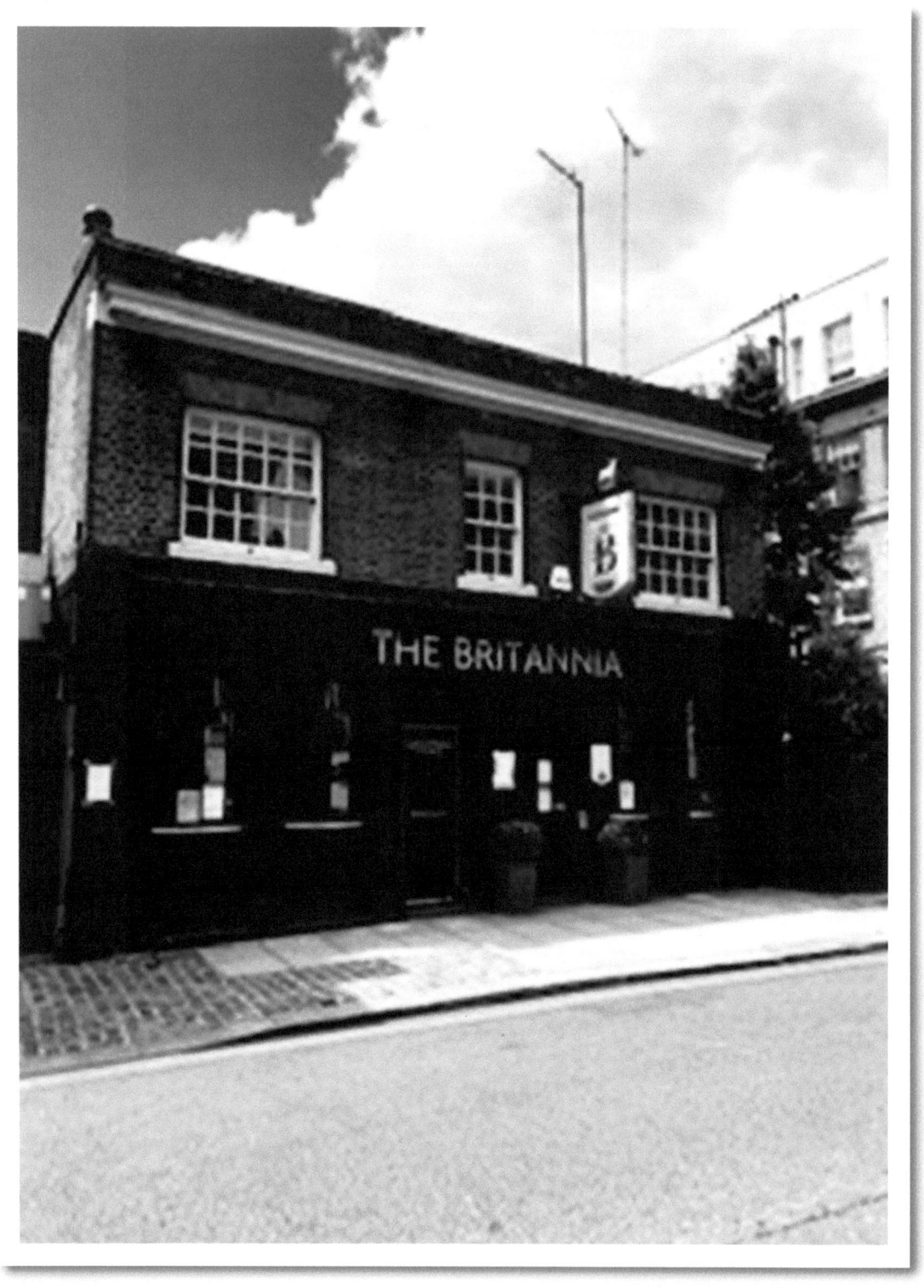

Britannia pub. Allen St. A favourite of mine.

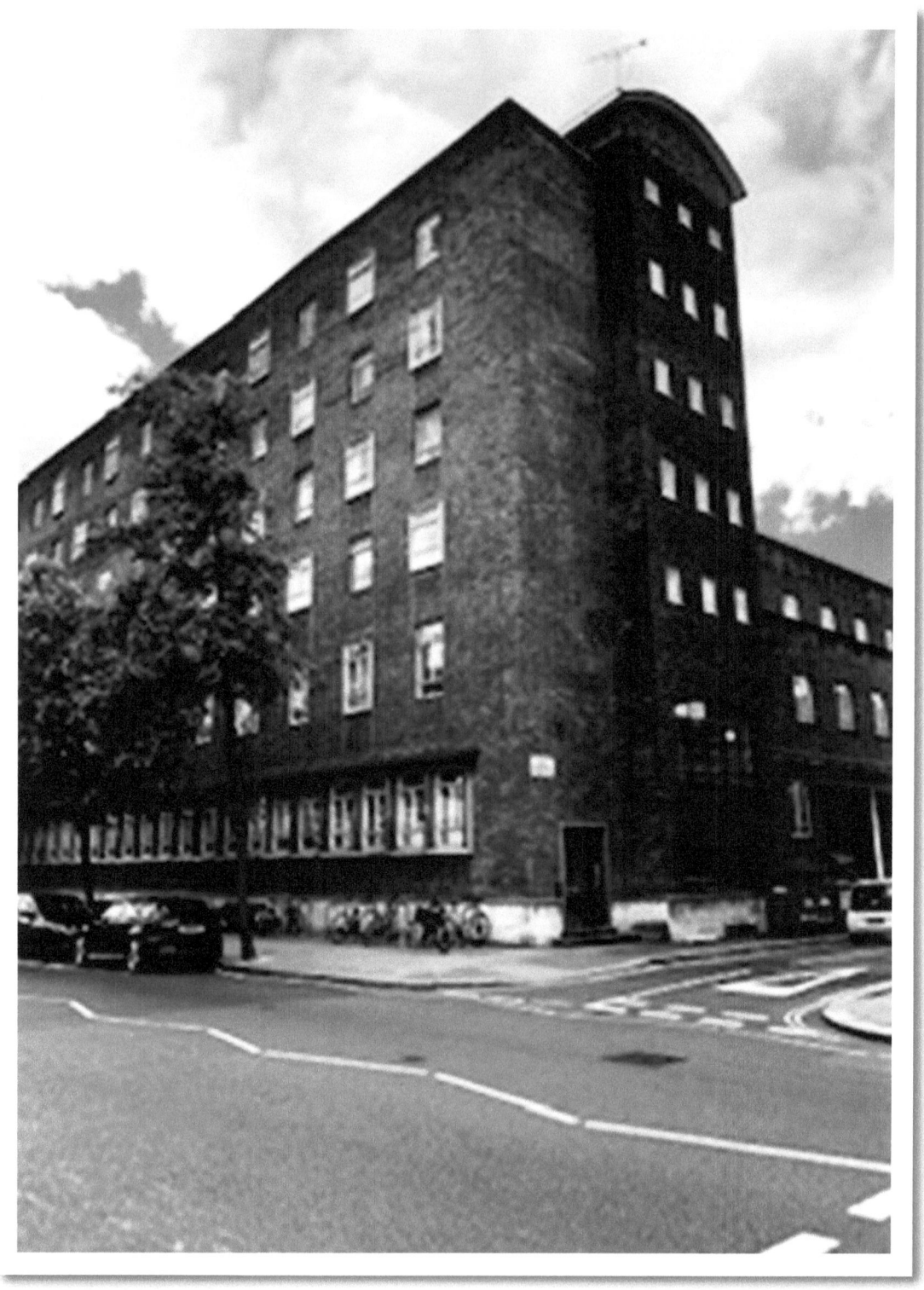

The Kensington Police Station. Above is accommodation provided for single policeman, where I lived after leaving Hendon Police Training School in January 1979. The living space is now defunct. Taken 14/05/20 1:00 pm.

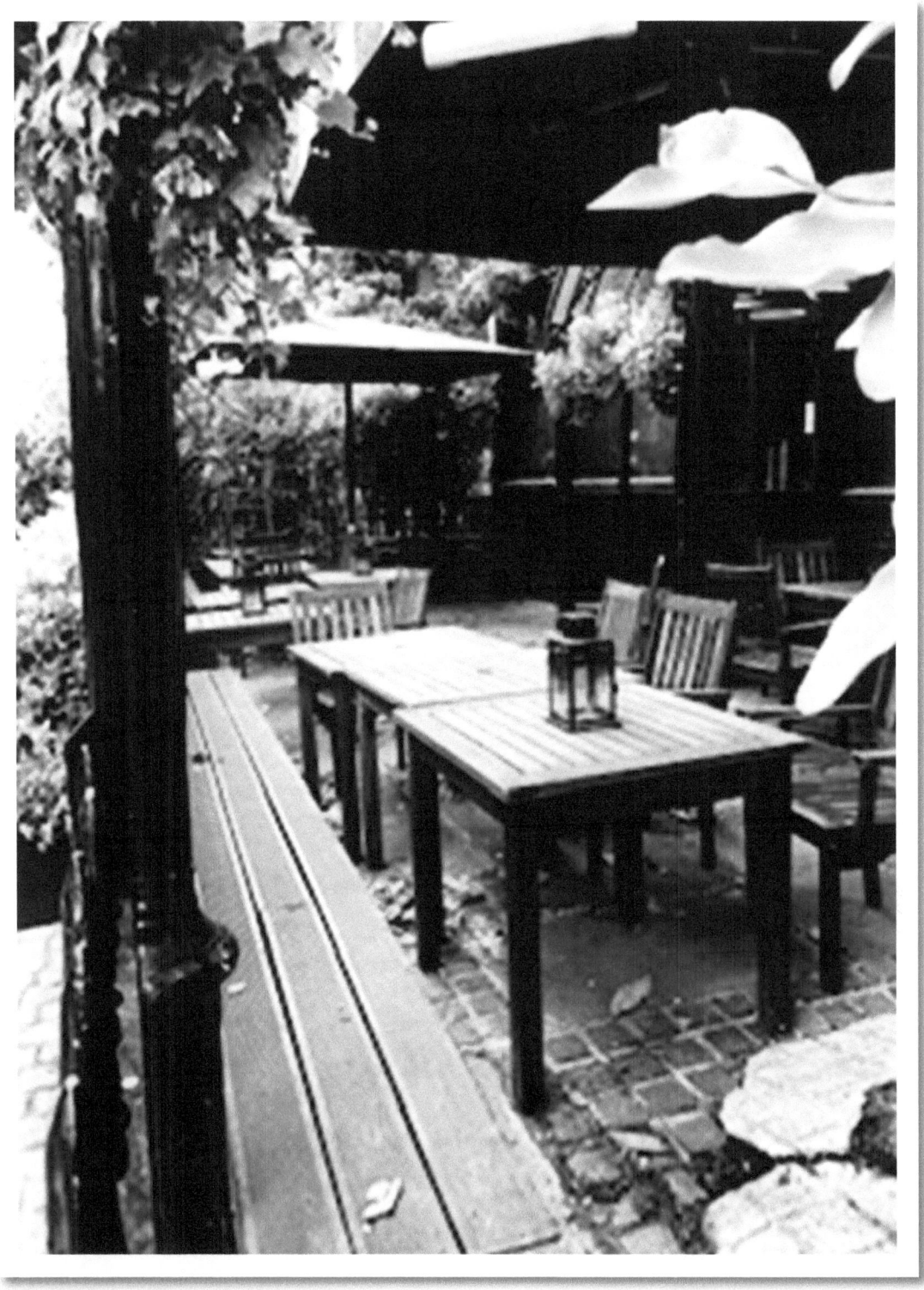

The beer garden of the Scarsdale pub at the rear of Kensington Police Station. Built circa 200 years ago apparently by Napoleonic Prisoners of War. Far too many hours of my life spent here. What can I say?

Taken 14/05/20 1:10 pm. Lockdown. Minus drinkers.

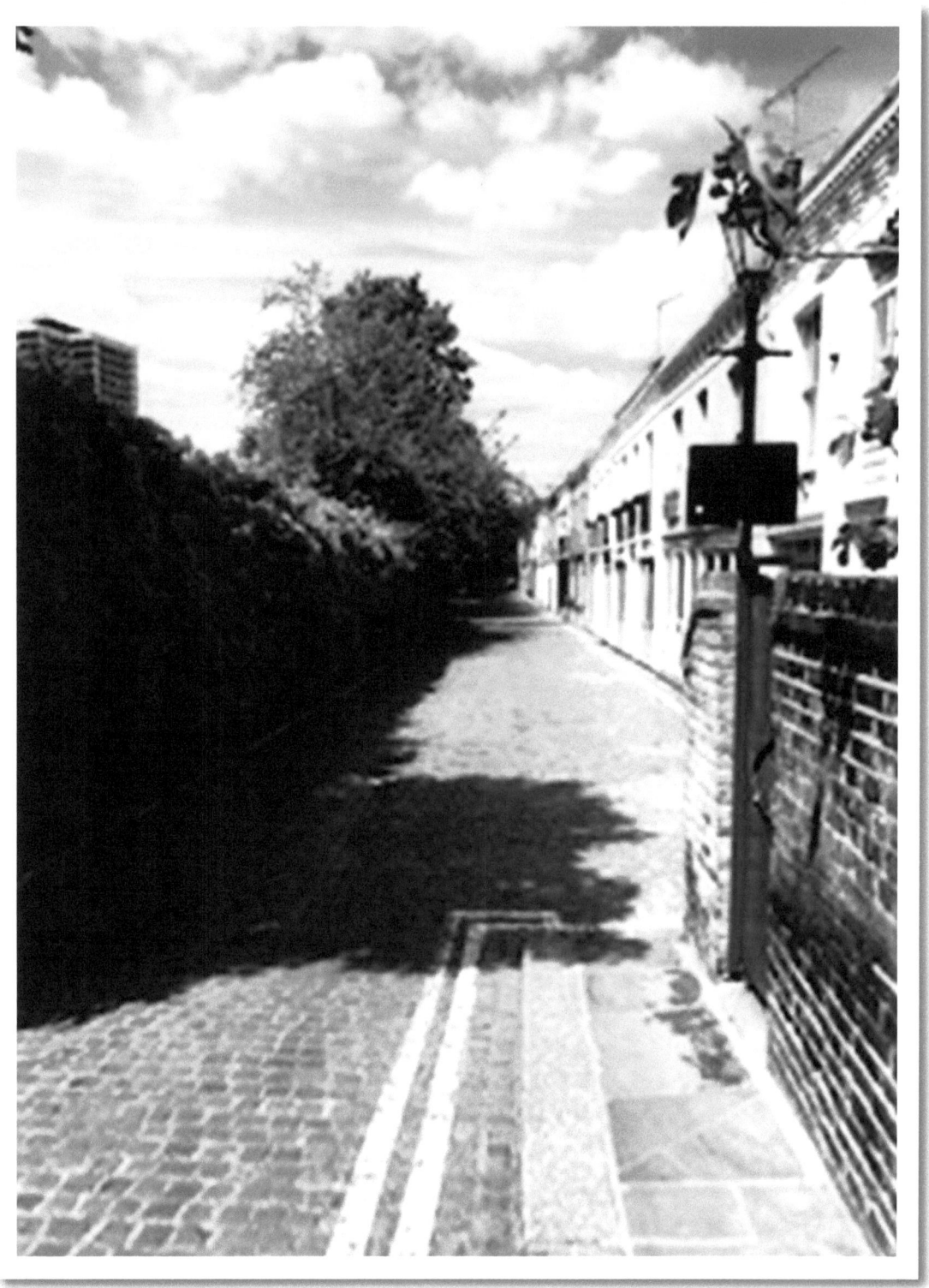

Hansard Mews W14. Near my Home. Classic example of a Mews in this part of town. Over the hedges is a railway line which is the only one that runs completely through the Capital. Kensington (Olympia) is just South of the mews. All other main line stations begin and end in London. Taken 20/05/20 1:00 pm.

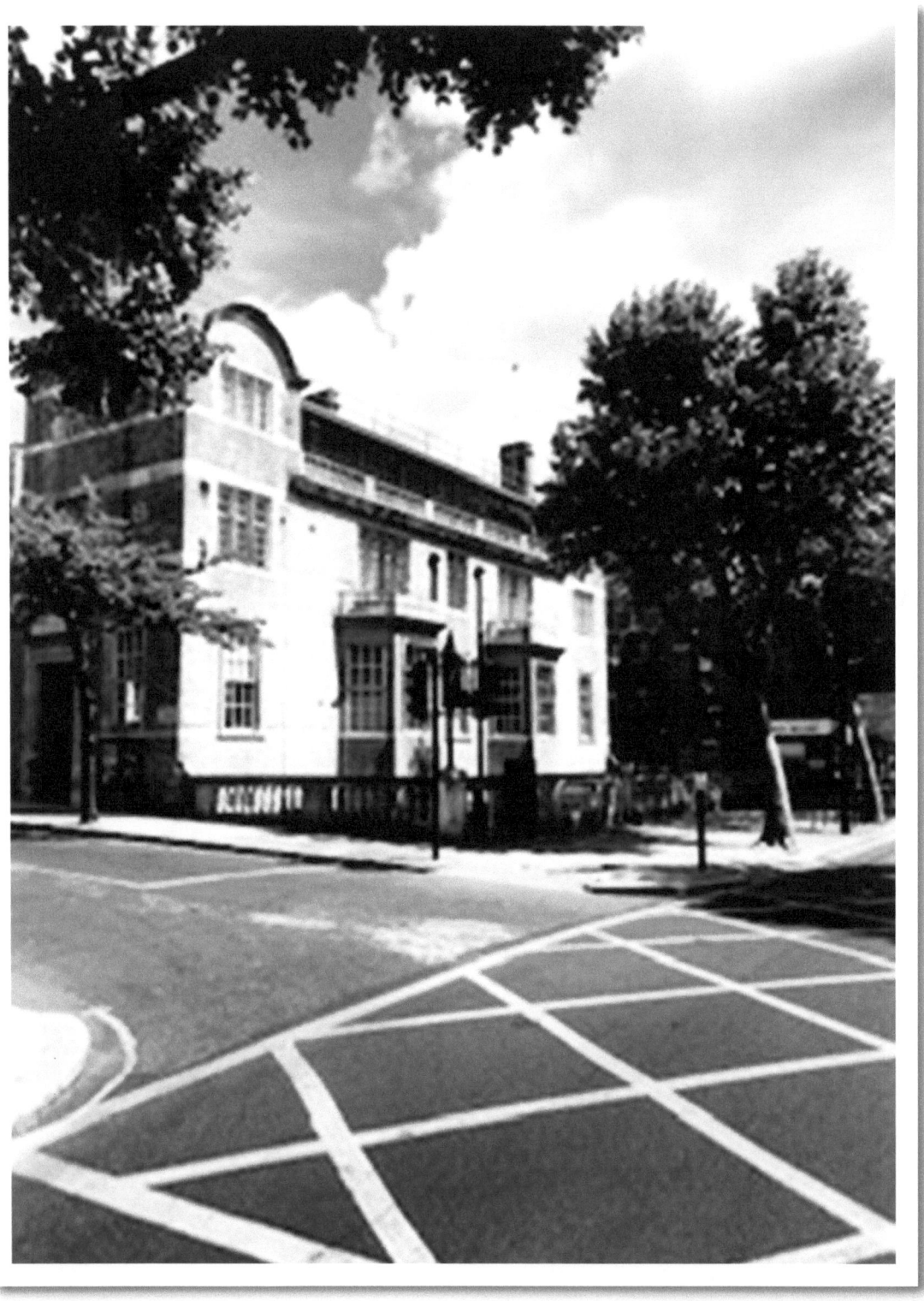

Notting Hill Police Station. Ladbroke Road junction with Ladbroke Grove W11. My first posting as an 18 and 10 month old Police Constable. Many memories & many friends. You always remember your 1st Station. Taken 15/05/20 2:15 pm.

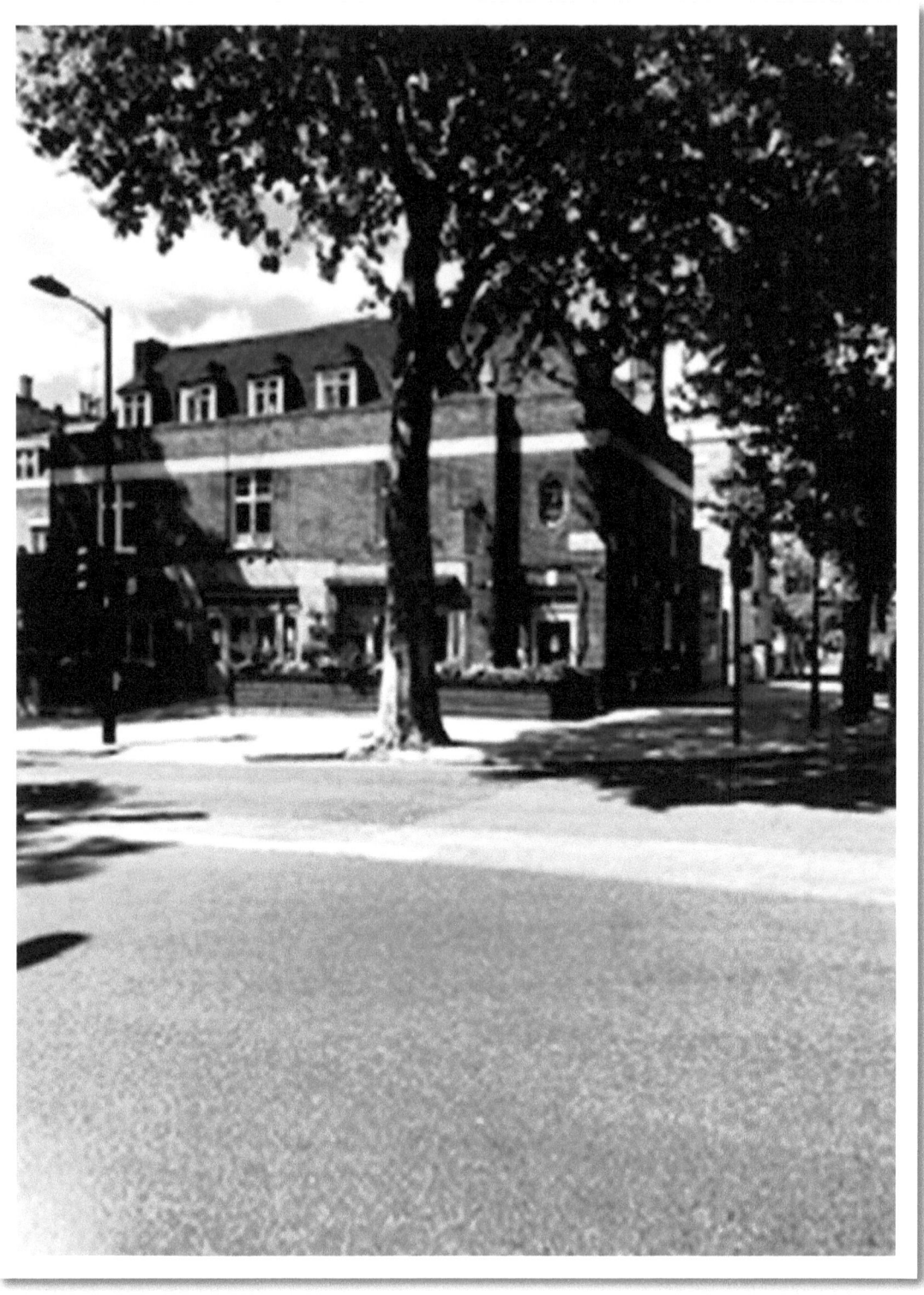

The Mitre Pub. Holland Park Avenue W11. A local boozer for Notting Hill officers. Regularly visited. Taken 15/05/20 2:20 pm.

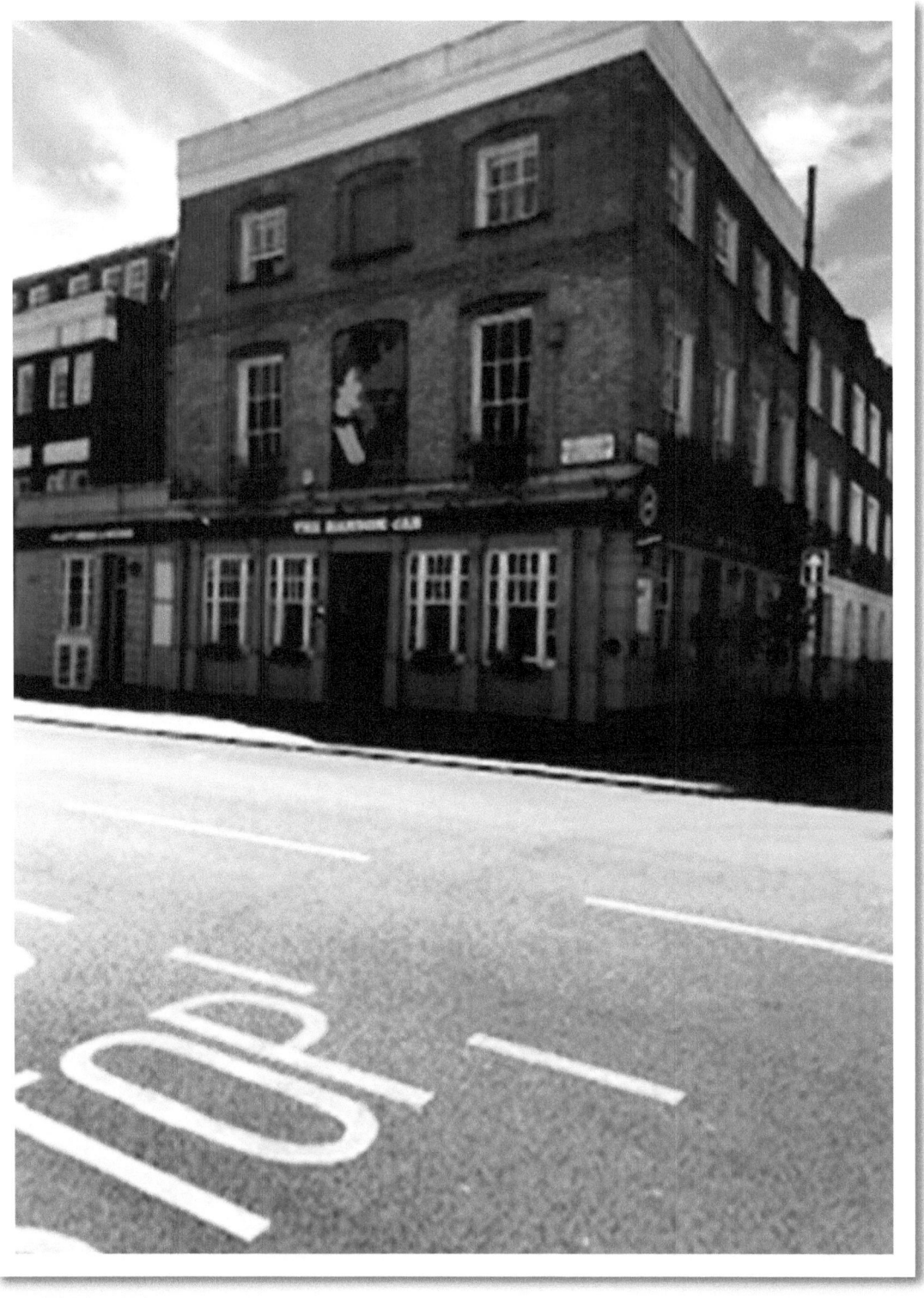

Hansom Cab Pub. I had my first pint here after checking in to the Section House.

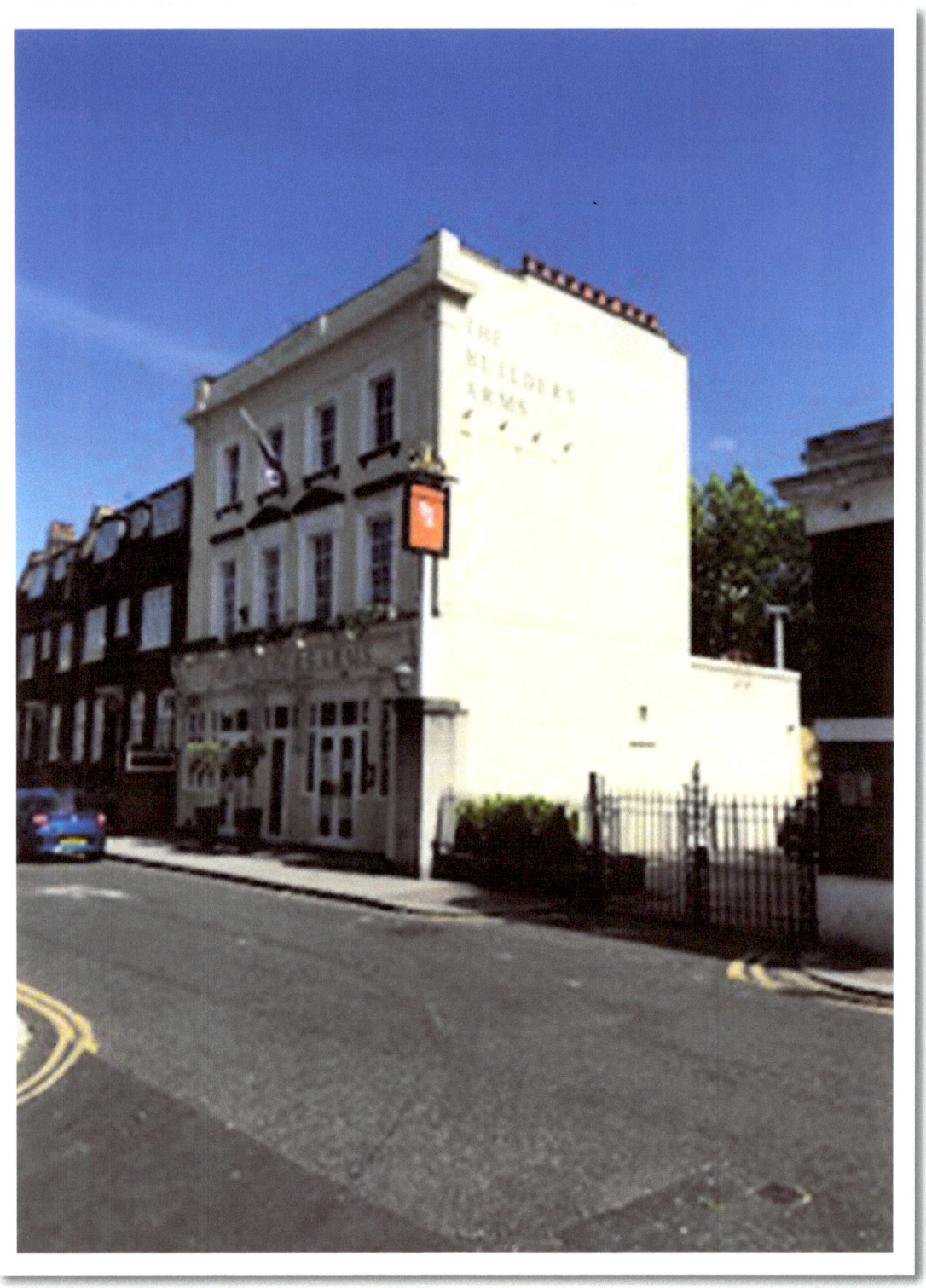

Builders Arms. Britten Street SW3. Well used local in my day to Chelsea Police.

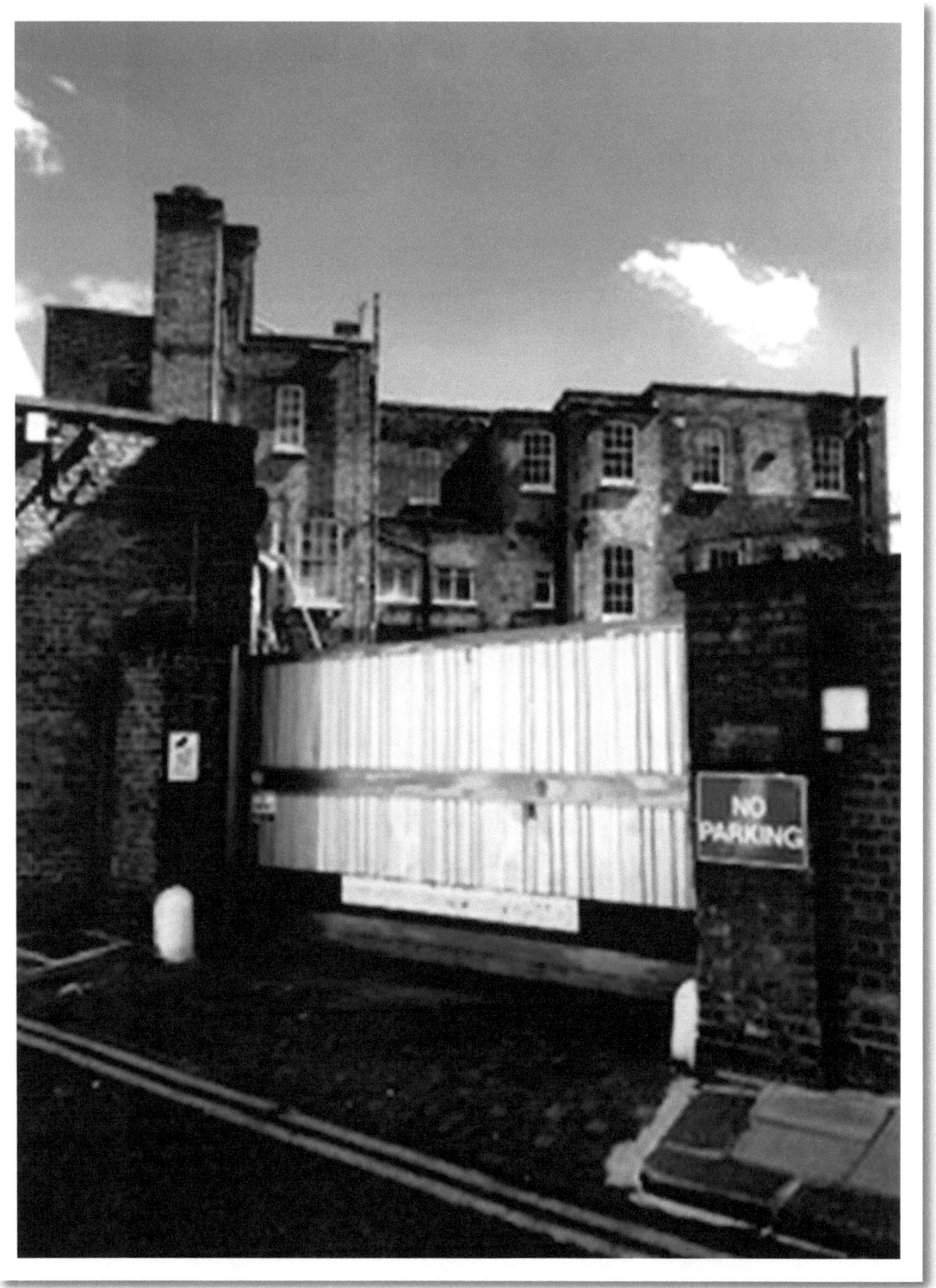

Rear gates of the Diplomatic Protection Group Yeomans Row. I was there for over 11years (1987-1998).

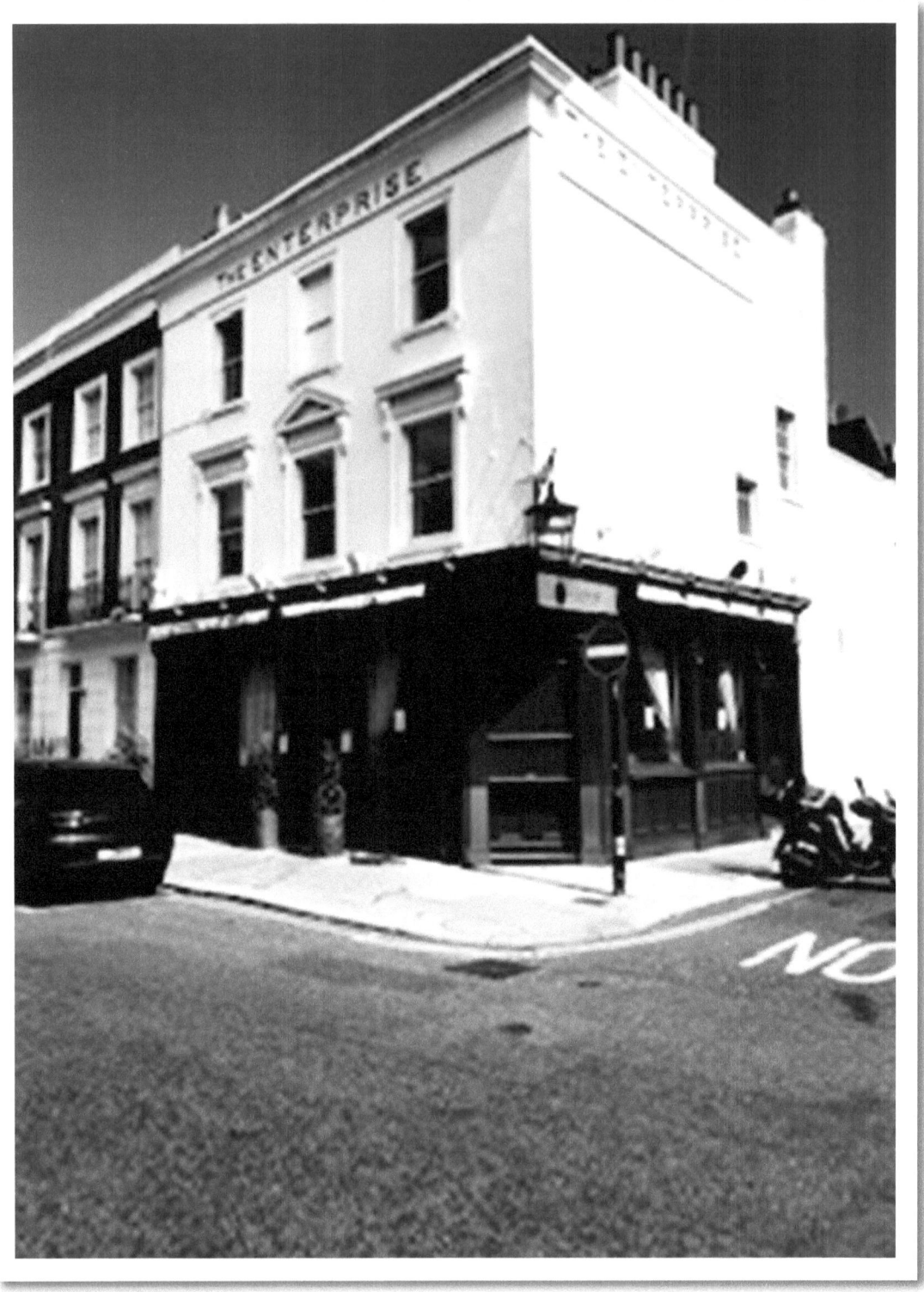

Enterprise Pub. Walton Street SW3. Well used, now a trendy bar & eatery.

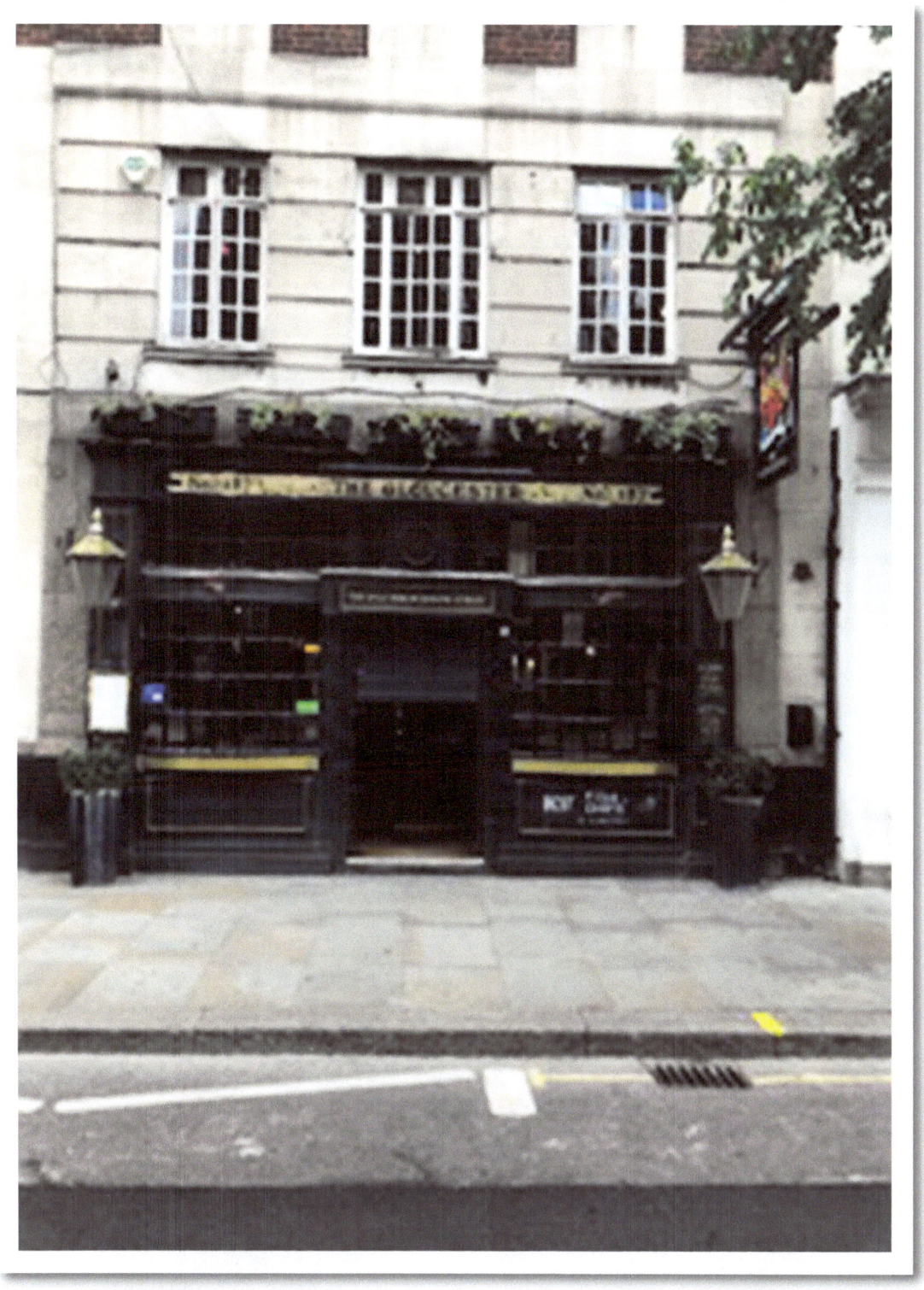

The Gloucester. Sloane Street. Knightsbridge. Lots of character.

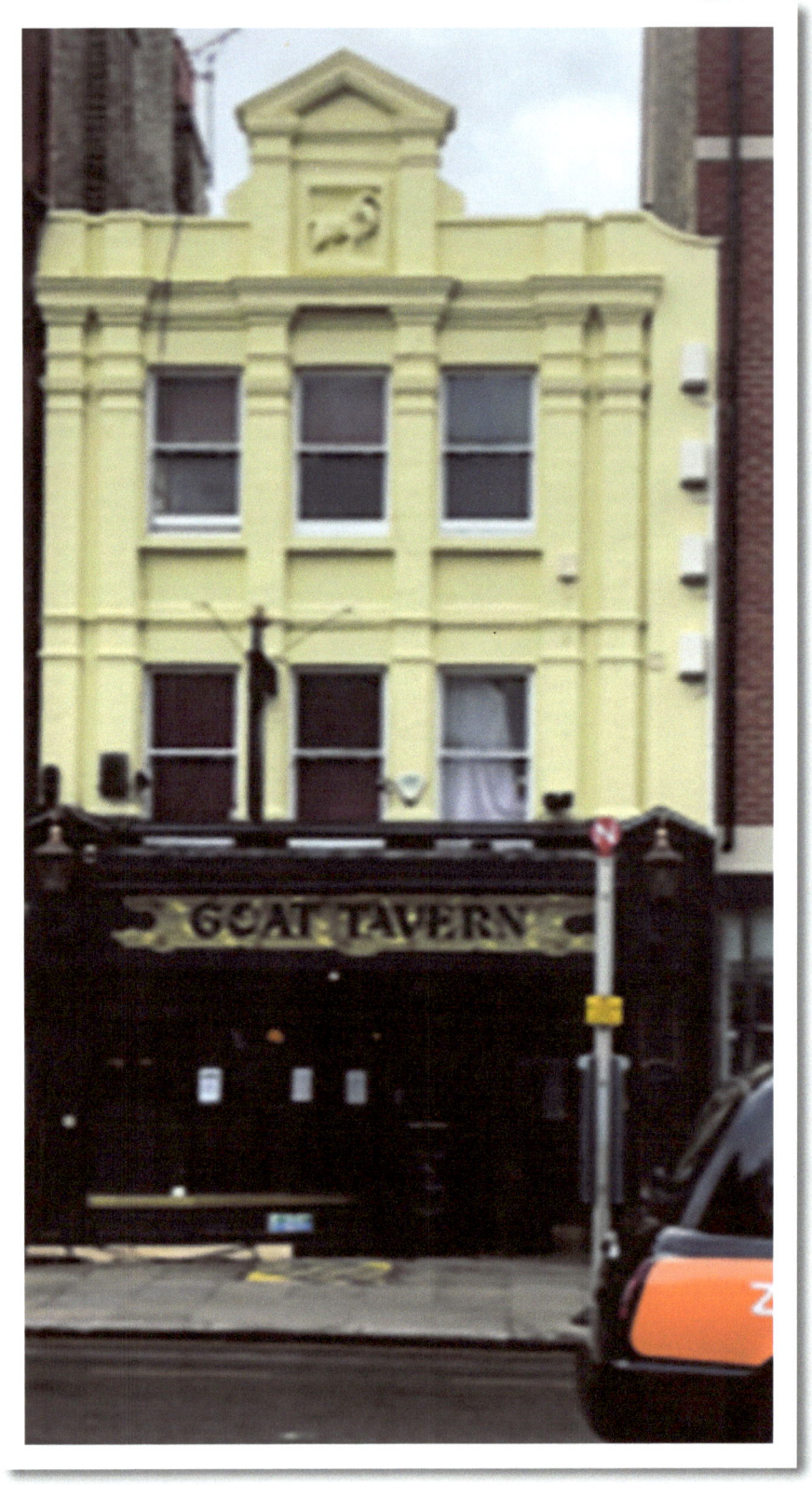

Goat Tavern. Only pub in Kensington High St. Tourist pub.

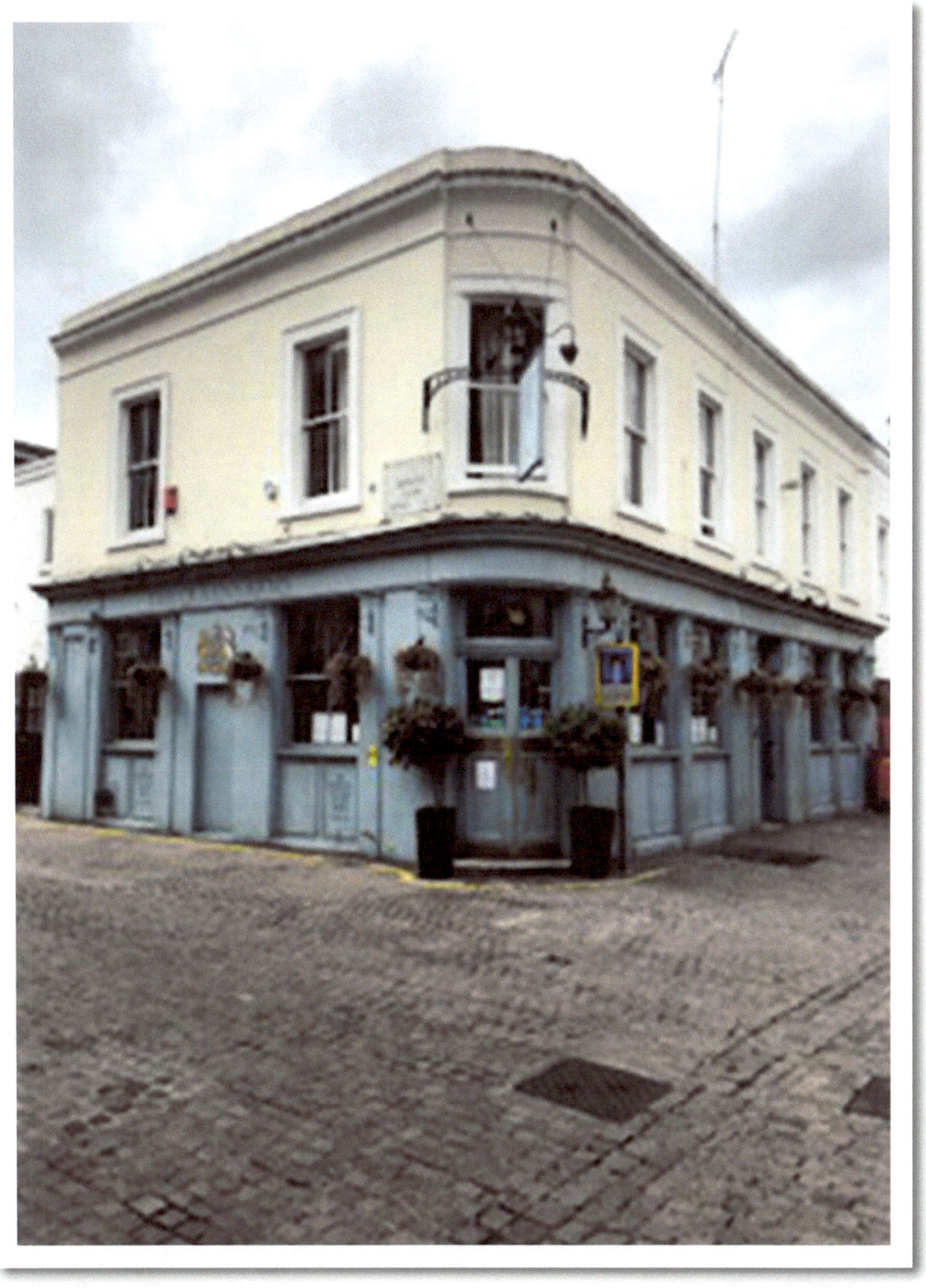

Queens Arms. Queens Gate Mews SW7. Used by Imperial College students. Hidden away.

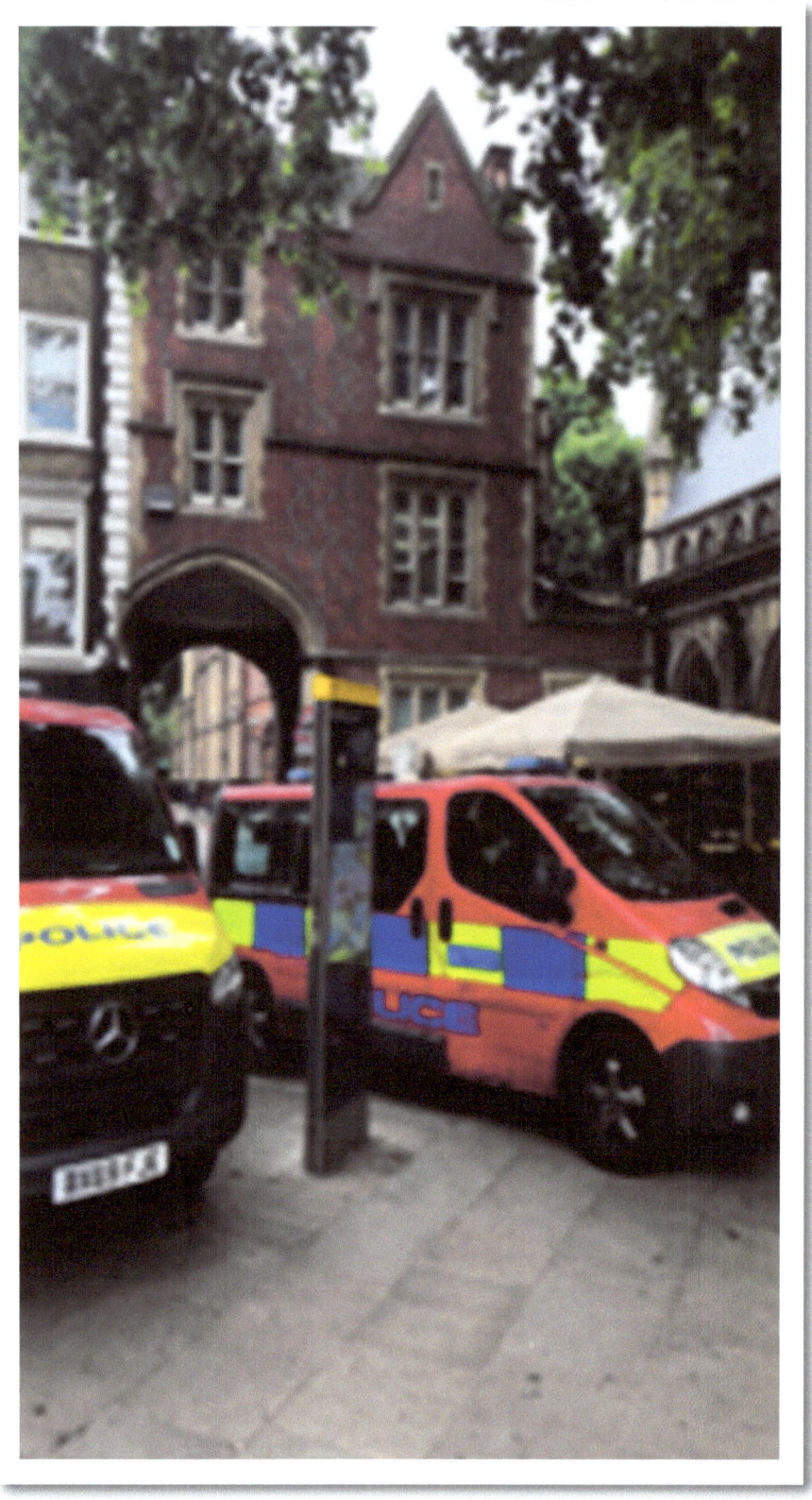

Kensington Diplomatic Protection base. Flower seller and Church adjacent.

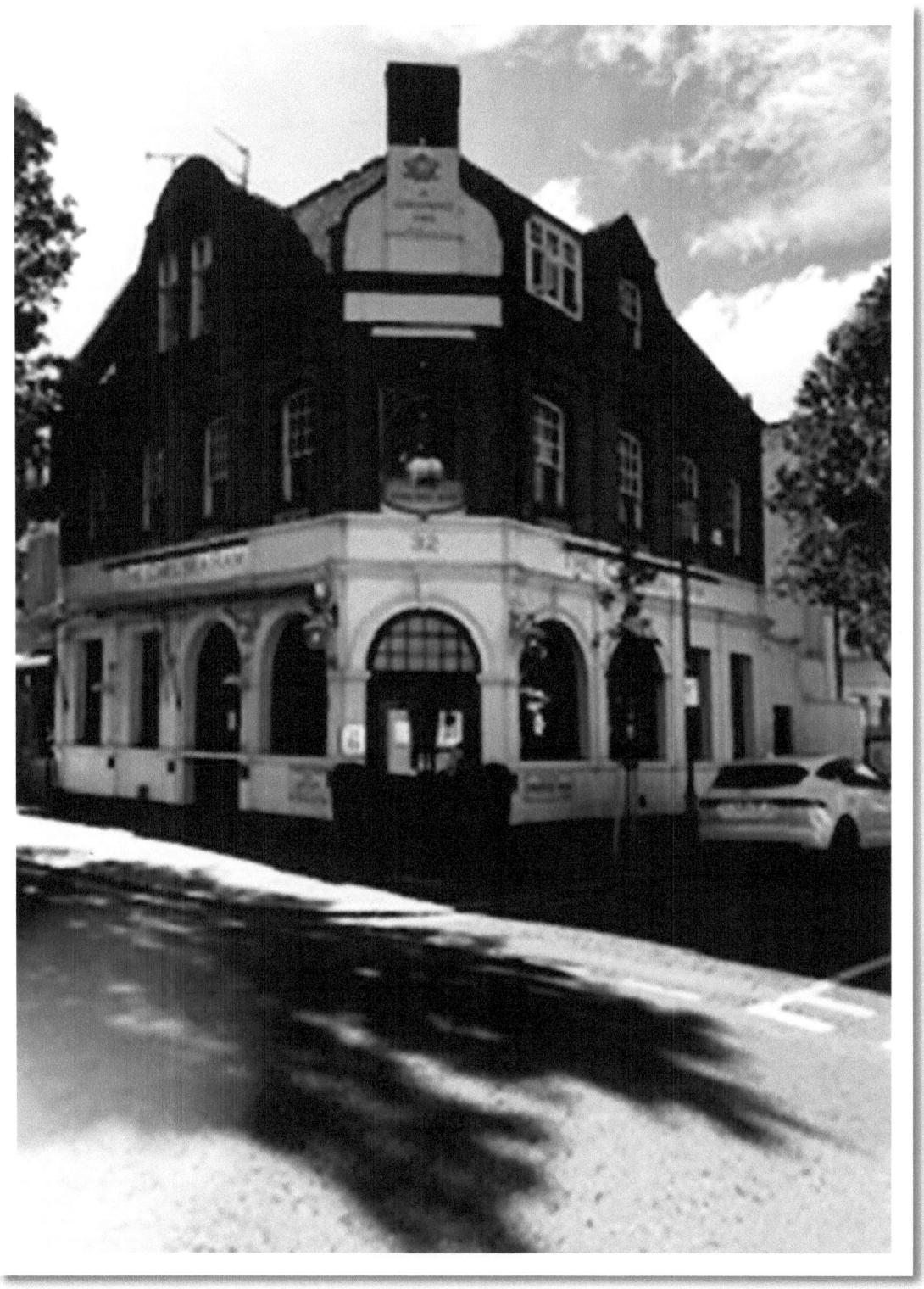

Chelsea Ram formerly the Ashburnham Arms. Burnaby Street SW10. Great local.

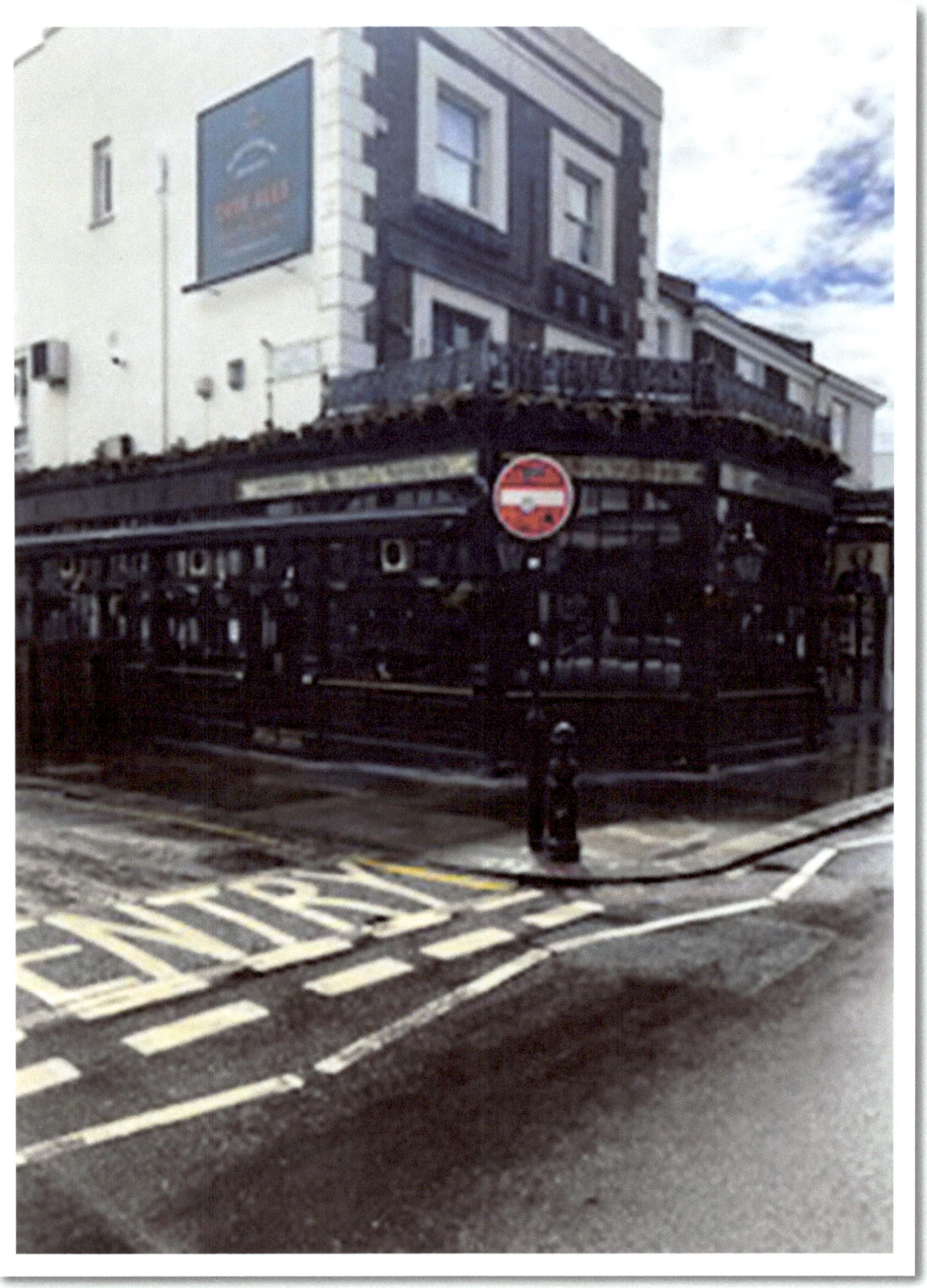

Chelsea Potter on the famous Kings Road. I've had one or two pints in there.

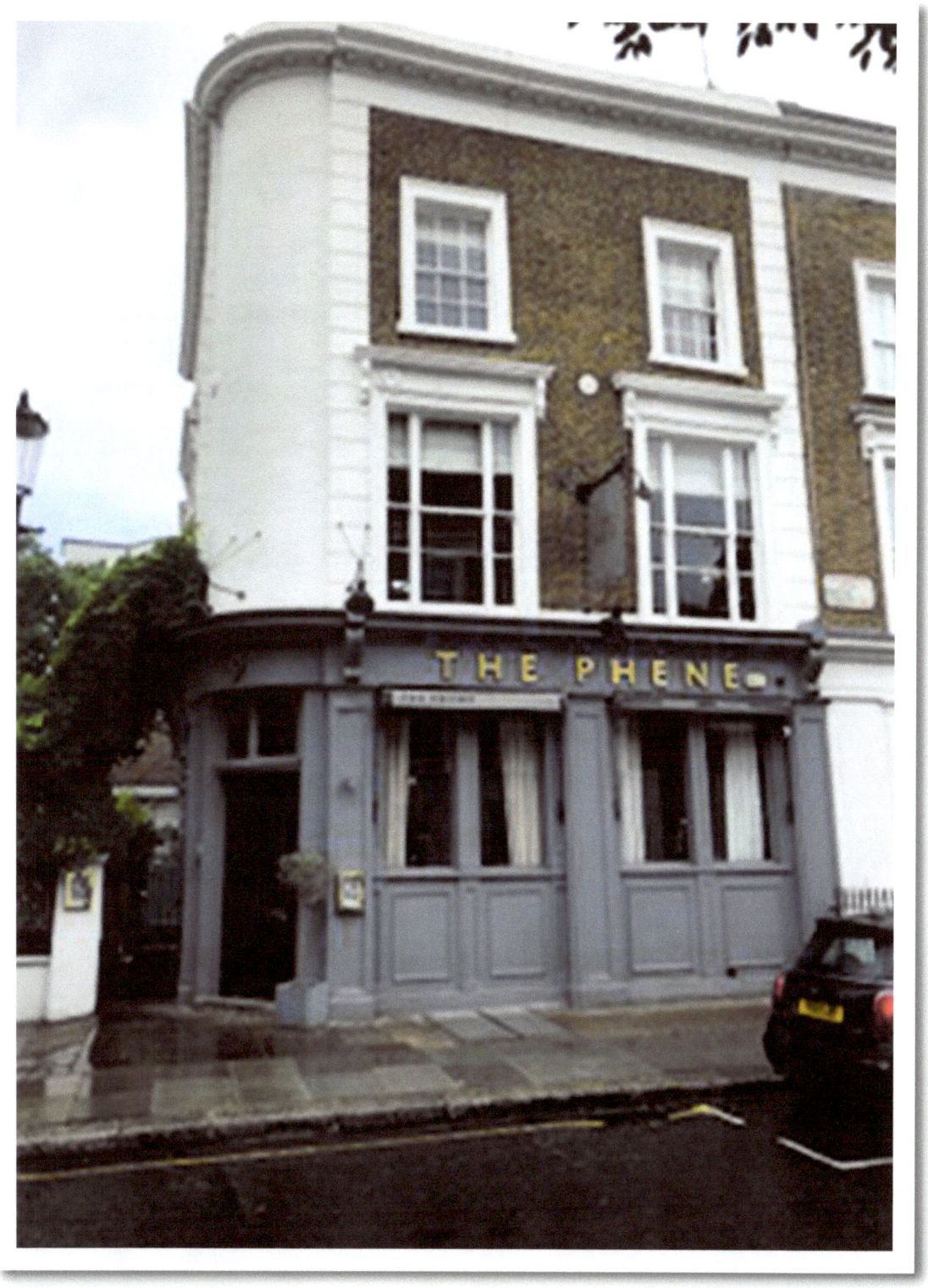

Phene Arms. Tucked away in Margaretta Terrace SW3. Haunt of George Best famous footballer.

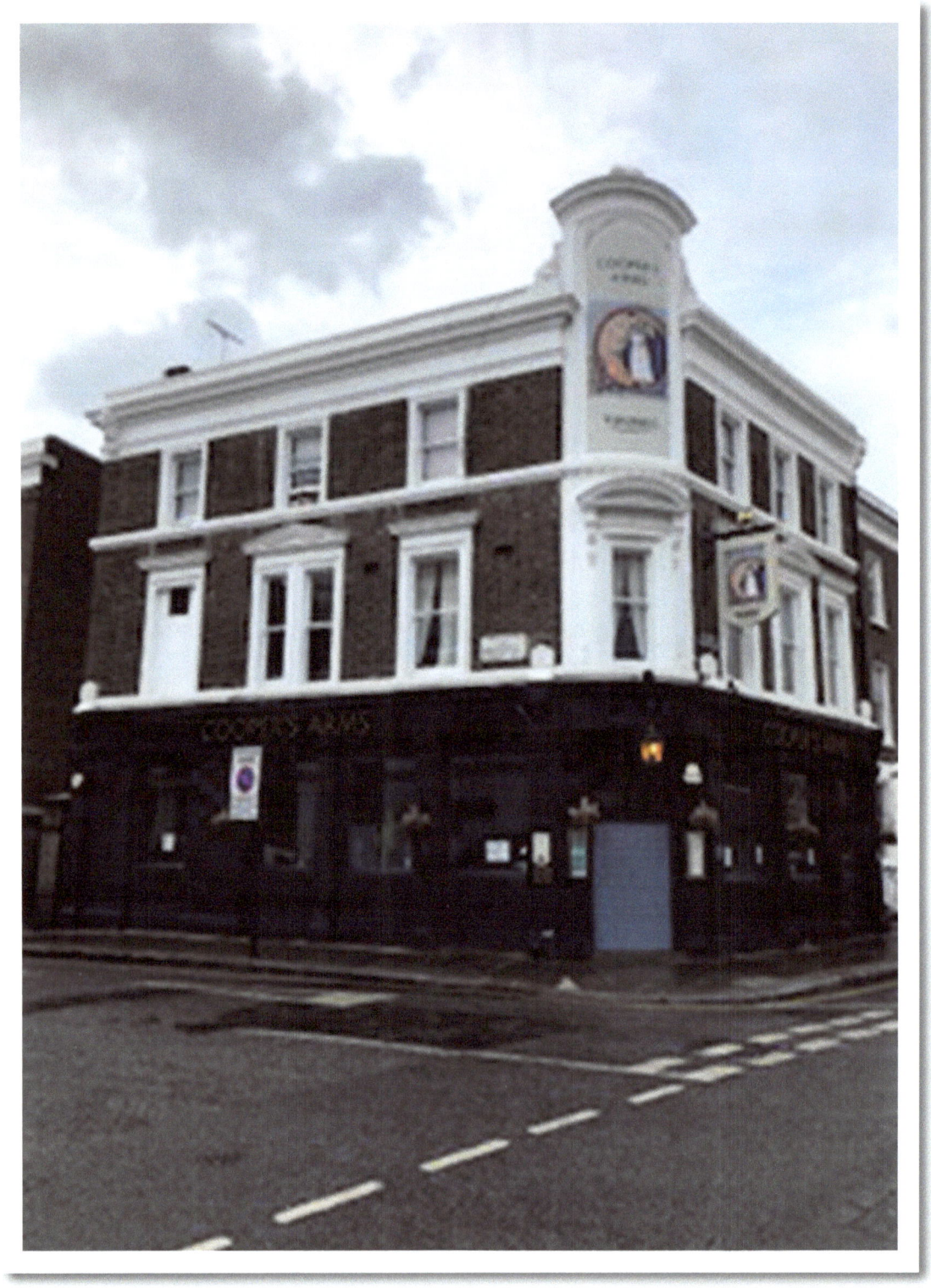

Coopers Arms. South off the Kings Road in Flood Street (Maggie Thatcher lived nearby). Tucked away...nice & quiet.

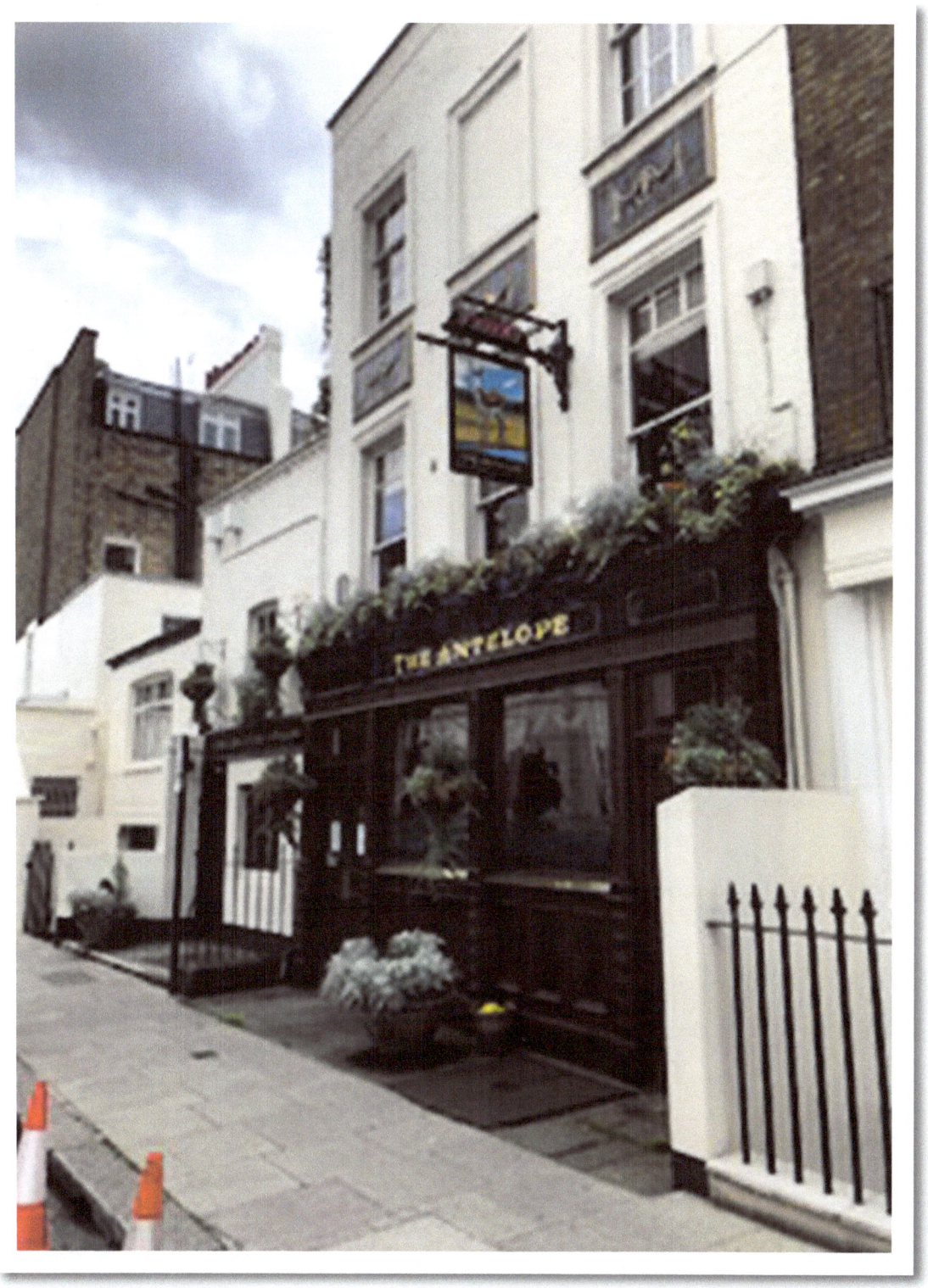

The Antelope. Right on the edge of the Royal Borough... Belgravia on the other side of the street. Been in here more than a few times.

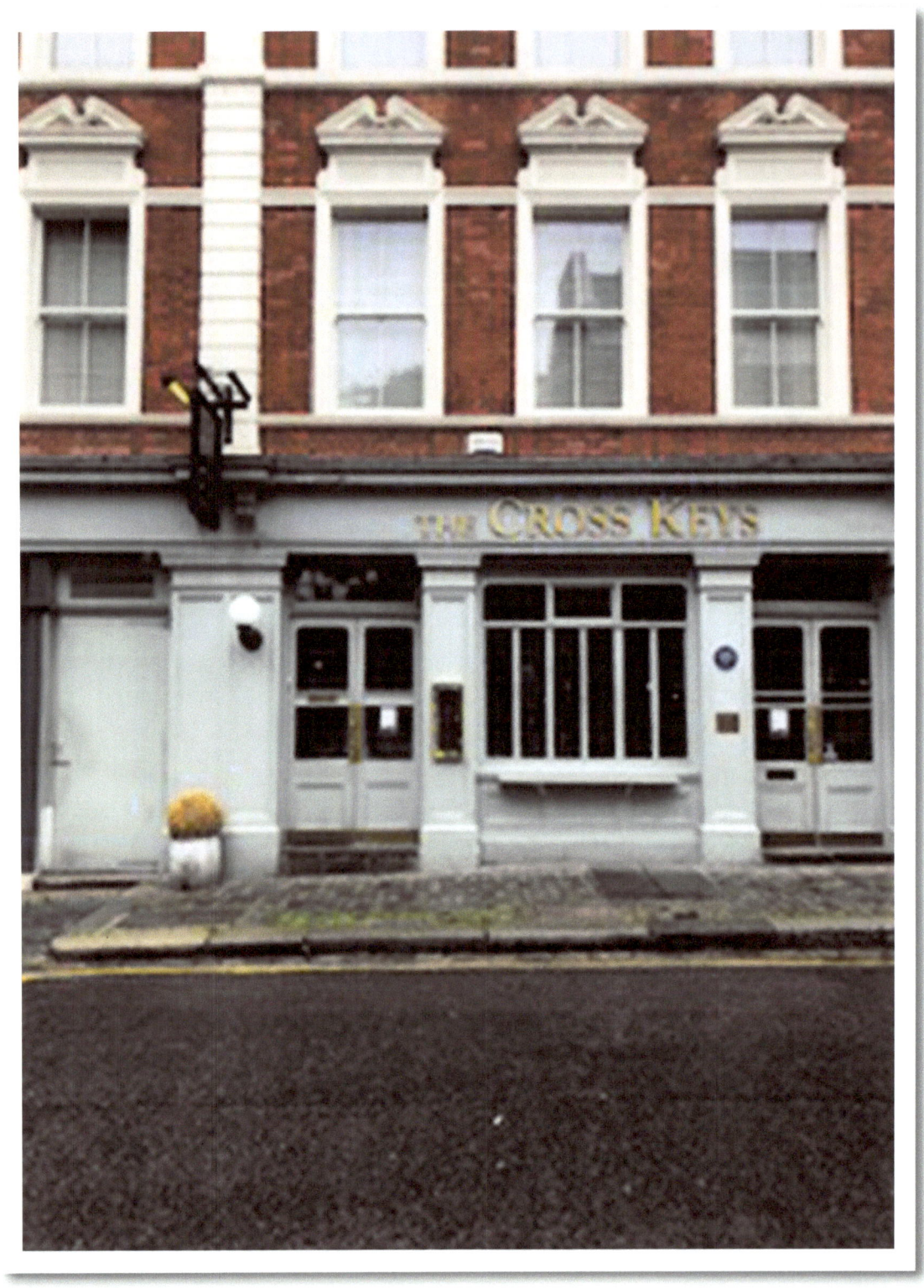

Just off the River. All the Cheyens.

About the Author

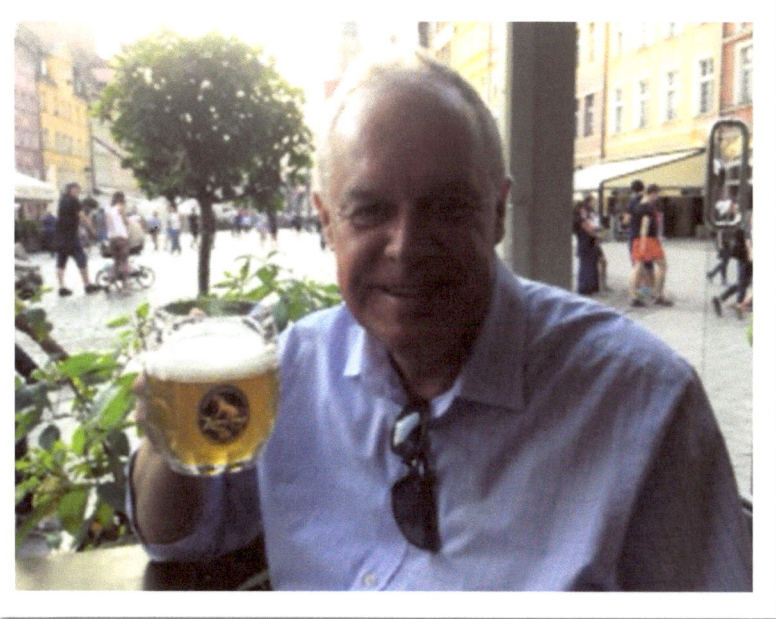

Born in the North East of England. I joined the Met Police Cadets at 16 (1976) and that became my life for the next 32 years all of in Central London a shift working Constable. Mostly in the Royal Borough of Kensington & Chelsea. Working at Notting Hill, Chelsea Police stations and later the Diplomatic Protection Group.

Later in retirement I got into local Conservative politics and stood as a Councilor candidate in the London Borough of 2014. Didn't get elected.

I'm married to Julia approaching 40 years have a daughter Charlotte and a son Jamie, both have flown the nest, also a Grandson Archer.

I've turned 60 this year (2020) I thought I'd try a few photographs with an IPhone!

www.ingramcontent.com/pod-product-compliance
Lightning Source LLC
Chambersburg PA
CBHW051823210526
45473CB00005B/1722